Six Fat Cubs

By Jamie Daniels

Illustrated by Joe Kulka

Target Skill Short Uu/u/

PEARSON

Scott Foresman

Six fat cubs are in a den.
Get up cubs!

Six fat cubs spot ten bees.

Six fat cubs run to the tree.

Six fat cubs jump up the tree.

Six fat cubs look at it.

Six fat cubs grab it.

Six fat cubs run!

Run to the den fast, fat cubs.